What's Inside

The lessons in this book were developed to be used with students to locate and use information about specific subjects.

The activity lessons can serve as a model for future research using the World Wide Web. Follow the format to create your own lessons to match your curriculum.

Activities Using the World Wide Web is divided into five sections:

This section addresses six topics using bookmarked Web sites.
Each topic is addressed with a set of three lessons:
- whole class activity—this lesson models the computer skills and techniques students are expected to use as they do the activity. You may want to hook your computer monitor to your classroom television with a video out cable so that students can see more easily. (Some additional hardware may be necessary.)
- small group activity—this lesson provides guided practice as students delve deeper into specific subject matter.
- individual activity—this lesson gives students independent practice as they report the information they have found.

Each lesson includes:
- step-by-step search directions
- addresses of related Web sites
- simplified student directions that can be displayed at the computer to help students work independently
- notetakers for lessons requiring them
- suggestions for *publishing* student work

Web Searches

This section explains effective search strategies and provides model lessons for doing a subject directory search and a keyword search.

Teaching Aids

To help make doing activities with the WWW easier, notetakers, templates checklists, parent letters, and patterns for student badges have been inc

WWW User Manual

Getting Teachers Started

Why Use the World Wide Web in the Classroom?

- The World Wide Web is up-to-date. Information on the World Wide Web can be updated as frequently as necessary, allowing students to access "real time" data such as weather satellite maps and space photographs.

- The World Wide Web is huge. Information on thousands of topics is distributed among different Web sites around the world so information on many topics is accessible to any web user.

- The World Wide Web is hypermedia. The Web presents multiple kinds of original information (text, images, videos, animations, and sounds) so that students with different learning styles can take advantage of different modes of information. They can explore text in a nonlinear way and establish their own path through this multimedia resource.

> As you're reading this tip section, check the glossary on pages 11 and 12 for any terms that you do not understand.

How Can the World Wide Web Enhance Instruction?

The World Wide Web is a rich resource for students and teachers. Using the WWW, you can:

- Take your class on an online field trip to a location you couldn't visit otherwise.
- View the latest up-to-date map of a specific place.
- Find news and information in a variety of foreign languages.
- View pictures from outer space.
- Read the latest news from dozens of well-known sources.
- Communicate and share ideas with others.
- Locate materials to enhance the work that your class is doing.
- Use the Web as a source for in-class materials.
- Research topics for the latest up-to-date information.
- Collect data about a given idea.
- Solve problems and participate in simulations.
- Look up lesson plans on specific topics.

Supervising Students on the Web

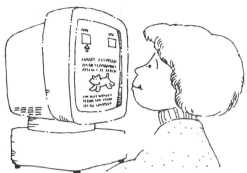

There is material on the World Wide Web that is inappropriate for kids to view. Parents, teachers, and students must work together to monitor and control the information that the students see.

Acceptable Use Policies

Most schools that provide access to the Internet for their students develop and implement an Acceptable Use Policy.

Such a policy will:

- make the rules of using the Internet clear to everyone — students, parents, administrators, and teachers

- provide guidance in case a student encounters inappropriate situations

- limit the school's legal liabilities

Several resources on the Web will help you develop Internet usage guidelines:

- http://www.tenet.edu/tenet-info/accept.html (a list of Acceptable Use Policies published by the Texas Education Network)

- http://www.missingkids.org/Safety guidelines are given under Internet Related Child Exploitation produced by The National Center for Missing and Exploited Children.

Keeping Parents and Students Informed

Creating the policy isn't meaningful unless parents and students understand the policy.

Explain your Acceptable Use Policy at a parent information night. Demonstrate uses of the Web and let parents use bookmarked sites to find information.

A sample letter for inviting parents to your *Using the Web Night* is included on page 4.

> Dear Parents,
>
> The Internet is a powerful and important tool. In our class we will be using the part of the Internet known as the World Wide Web. The World Wide Web is a place where text, pictures, sound, and videos on an amazing array of topics are stored and made accessible to computers around the world. As we do research we will consult the electronic resources of the World Wide Web, as well as traditional print resources.
>
> Please come to a Web Information Night to see how we will be using the Web in our classroom.
>
> - You'll see a sample project.
> - You'll use a bookmarked site to find information yourself.
> - You'll find out about our Acceptable Use Policy.
>
> Thank you,
>
> When?_____
>
> Where?_____

Dear Parents,

The Internet is a powerful and important tool. In our class we will be using the part of the Internet known as the World Wide Web. The World Wide Web is a place where text, pictures, sound, and videos on an amazing array of topics are stored and made accessible to computers around the world. As we do research we will consult the electronic resources of the World Wide Web, as well as traditional print resources.

Please come to a Web Information Night to see how we will be using the Web in our classroom.

- You'll see a sample project.

- You'll use a bookmarked site to find information yourself.

- You'll find out about our Acceptable Use Policy.

Thank you,

When?_____

Where?_____

Dear Parents,

The Internet is a powerful and important tool. In our class we will be using the part of the Internet known as the World Wide Web. The World Wide Web is a place where text, pictures, sound, and videos on an amazing array of topics are stored and made accessible to computers around the world. As we do research we will consult the electronic resources of the World Wide Web, as well as traditional print resources.

Please come to a Web Information Night to see how we will be using the Web in our classroom.

- You'll see a sample project.

- You'll use a bookmarked site to find information yourself.

- You'll find out about our Acceptable Use Policy.

Thank you,

When?_____

Where?_____

Using the World Wide Web for Research

Because it is important to model the use of a tool for students before expecting them to work in small groups or independently, the lessons in this book present a whole class demonstration lesson, a small group research lesson, and then an individual research lesson on each topic addressed. Every lesson moves through the following four steps:

1. Find information.

- Students begin by using preselected open sites,

- Progress to using bookmarked sites,

- And then use links to additional sites.

Note: The lessons in this book do not involve free exploration by students.

2. Evaluate the information.

Teachers and students use a checklist to determine whether a site has valid, up-to-date, understandable information.

3. Take notes on the information.

Students read information, determine what is important to remember, and record keywords on notetakers.

4. Present the information to others.

Students use the information on their notetakers to create:

- oral reports
- written reports
- multimedia presentations

Before any activity using the World Wide Web:
- Make sure that the URLs you plan to use are valid. URLs can change.
- Preload the materials into the disk cache if possible.

In case you are unable to connect to the Net or the web site is "down," have a backup plan:

- print resources   • filmstrip   • periodicals

Updated information on the sites referenced in this book can be found at http://www.evan-moor.com. Click on the *Product Updates* link.

Reporting on Web Research

Traditional Reports

The templates included in this book can be used for written reports or as prompts for oral reports.

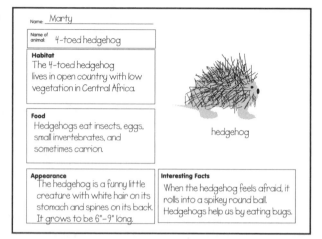

Reports Prepared on the Computer

Scan the templates into your computer and have students use a drawing and word processing program like KID PIX® to fill in the template. Student directions for this type of report are given in each lesson. Make sure that your students are familiar with the tools and the operations that they will need to use. For additional information and lessons that teach students to use the writing and drawing tools, see other books in the *Teaching and Learning with the Computer Series* shown on the back cover.

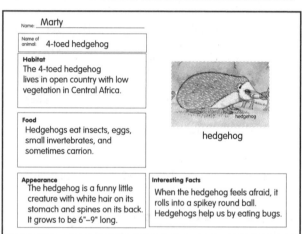

Multimedia Projects

Project 1— Creating a Computer Slide Show Using Student Work

A slide show is a multimedia presentation. It is a way to view a series of computer report templates using the computer. The computer simply flashes one report after another onto the screen.

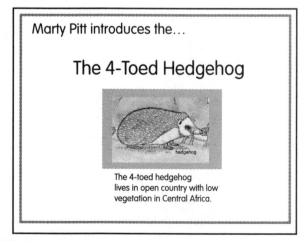

Steps to follow*:

1. Open the slide show tool in your program.

2. Choose a saved picture.

3. Put the saved picture into the first frame of the slide show.

4. Continue to put saved pictures in order.

5. Choose the musical transition you would like and the time each slide should remain on the screen.

6. Add recorded descriptions or sound effects.

7. Save your show.

8. Play the show and enjoy it. (Select the looped feature to see it play again and again without stopping.)

* Note: Check the manual for the program you are using for any variation from the procedure given here.

Project 2— **Create a Multimedia Presentation**

Use the information on your notetaker to create a multimedia program, using computer software such as Hyperstudio® or Digital Chisel®. You will be able to access any part of the presentation at any time. You can move in sequential or random order as you click on buttons to move to any screen in the program.

Check your program manual for specific instructions.

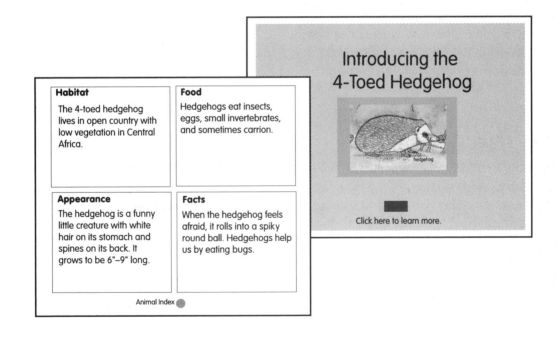

Habitat

The 4-toed hedgehog lives in open country with low vegetation in Central Africa.

Food

Hedgehogs eat insects, eggs, small invertebrates, and sometimes carrion.

Appearance

The hedgehog is a funny little creature with white hair on its stomach and spines on its back. It grows to be 6"–9" long.

Facts

When the hedgehog feels afraid, it rolls into a spiky round ball. Hedgehogs help us by eating bugs.

Animal Index

Introducing the
4-Toed Hedgehog

hedgehog

Click here to learn more.

Evaluating Web Sites

Just as users of print materials must evaluate the source of their information, it is up to the users of the World Wide Web to be critical consumers of information.

As a teacher, it is your job to find the materials, out of the thousands of sites available, that can be useful to you as an educator. The Web contains a wealth of wonderful resources, but it also contains a great deal of misinformation and unevaluated information. So evaluate a Web site just as you would carefully evaluate a print resource. And remember, since Web resources can change so quickly, evaluating them is an ongoing process.

Before you bookmark a site for use with your class, consider the quality of the site.

- Is the site technically reliable?
- Is the site objective and accurate?

An evaluation checklist is provided for you on page 9. "Yes" answers to the checklist questions indicate a high-quality Web page. Add additional questions to the checklist so that the list will meet the needs of your classroom.

Remember that hypertext links may lead the user to web pages of a different quality. Evaluate each Web page independently.

Each time your class visits a new site, take the time to discuss the evaluation that you previously did. Model the evaluation for your class, discussing each step and defining the criteria in terms that they can understand. A sample of how you might model a Web page evaluation is given on page 15.

Checklist for Evaluating Web Sites

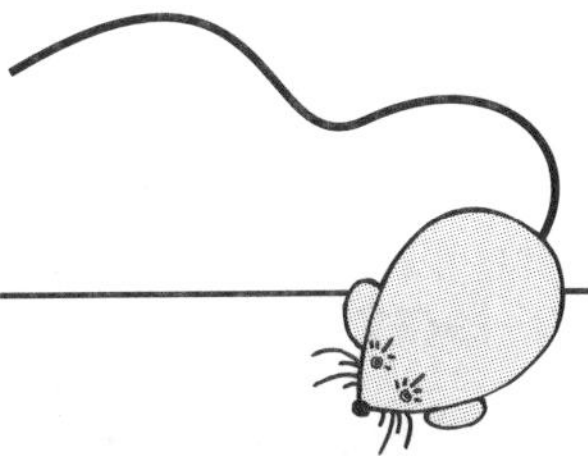

Site URL:

Where did the information come from?

Is it clear who sponsors the page?	yes	no
Is the purpose of the sponsoring organization given?	yes	no
Is the author of the information given?	yes	no
Are the author's qualifications stated?	yes	no

Is the information accurate?

Are the sources of any factual information listed?	yes	no
Is the information free from grammatical, spelling, and other errors?	yes	no
Are charts and graphs clearly labeled and easy to read?	yes	no

Is the information objective?

Is the information presented as a public service?	yes	no
Is the information free of advertising?	yes	no
Is the information trying to change the opinion of the audience?	yes	no

Is the information current?

Are there dates on the page to tell when it was written?	yes	no
Does the page tell when it was last updated?	yes	no

Is the information complete?

Is the page complete? (not under construction)	yes	no
Are the topics included explored in depth?	yes	no

Is the information appropriate?

Is the design of the site easy to understand?	yes	no
Is the material understandable?	yes	no

For Your Information as You Evaluate Web Pages

Six Basic Types of Web Pages

- **Reference/Informational Web Page** —The purpose of an information Web page is to present factual information. The URL often ends in .edu or .gov since many of the sites are sponsored by educational institutions or government agencies. The information is much like printed reference materials — encyclopedias, nonfiction reference books, atlases, dictionaries, research reports, and nature guides.

- **Entertainment**—A site designed for fun. Entertainment sites often include interactive games or online music and videos.

- **Business/Marketing**—Sites designed to represent specific products or sponsored by commercial companies are considered commercial web pages. These URLs often include the abbreviations .com or .org. While their ultimate goal is selling, some business/marketing sites can present excellent information. In addition, you will find some sites that blend entertainment, information, and advertising in an "infommerical" page. View these Web pages with the same critical eye you would an infommercial.

- **News** — Like news radio stations or news television networks, news sites present the latest happenings around the world.

- **Advocacy** — Sites sponsored by groups representing and promoting a specific viewpoint. Information presented tends to represent only one side.

- **Personal** — Individual home pages fall in the category of personal sites. Information on these pages can be good but should be verified for accuracy.

To Make Your Job Easier

You may want to take advantage of the work of others who have developed systems for evaluating Web resources and who report their findings online. Three evaluation sites are listed below:

http://www.gsn.org/links/index.html

The Global School house provides this databank of educational links submitted and evaluated by educators.

http://ww.kn.pacbell.com/wired/bluewebn/

This is a searchable database of outstanding Internet learning sites. A rubic is given for site evaluation.

http://www.navigator.tufts.edu/educator.html

Nutritional Web sites are reviewed by Tufts University nutritionalists. Sites are reviewed and updated quarterly.

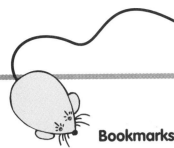

Glossary of WWW Terms

Bookmarks (Favorites)—a way to save the location of a Web site.

To mark a site so that it can be found again quickly, select Add Bookmark from the Bookmarks menu. (In Internet Explorer select Add to Favorites from the Favorites menu.) To revisit the site, select the name of the site from the bookmark (favorite) menu.

Cache—the way that your browser stores text, pictures, and other information from the Web.

If an item is in the cache, it can be loaded much more quickly from your own computer than it can from the network.

Frames—the way that Web authors organize the information that appears on a page.

If you're having trouble navigating through a Web site, use the pop-up menu for help.

Note: To display the pop-up menu on the Macintosh, just hold down the mouse button over the page. To display the pop-up menu in Windows, right-click the mouse over the page.

Images (Graphics)—pictures that appear on Web pages.

Sometimes only illustrations, graphics may also be links to other locations.

Internet—a global computer network that connects government institutions, commercial organizations, schools, and people together to share information.

It has been in existence in one form or another for more than two decades. It is a network infrastructure of computers around the world that allows users to share information with each other.

Links (Hyperlinks)—items that, when clicked, lead to another Web page.

Links are sometimes underlined words that are a different color from the rest of the text on a page. They can also be icons or small pictures. When the mouse is held over a link and clicked, the browser moves to the linked Web page.

Link History—a list of your most recent actions in a Web session.

If you use the Back and Forward buttons on the tool bar, you'll move up and down in the history list.

Relevance—The results of a search are ranked by their similarity to the search terms.

When the list of "hits" is presented, it is ranked for relevancy. The search engine's indexing software has chosen sites that most closely meet the query.

Results of search engines are usually given numeric scores that let you gauge the relative relevance of each document. Relevance is often measured in percentages. (100% is a perfect match.)

Search Engine—Search engines are enormous indexes of information locations that have been gathered by computer programs designed to automatically find sources of information.

Different search engines vary in speed, options, and how documents are indexed.

Search Terms—the words defining the topic you are searching for.

If you want information on the "right whale," your search terms should be "right whale." Using only "whale" will not define the search adequately.

URL (Uniform Resource Locator)—a unique address that identifies the location of a document on the World Wide Web.

An URL is like a telephone number. You "dial" the URL to talk to the Web site you're looking for. The URL is found in the location field (address bar) at the top of the window of a Web page. URLs must be correctly typed.

Web Browser—the software you launch on your computer to access and retrieve information from the Web.

As of this printing, two of the most common Web browsers are Netscape Navigator and Microsoft Internet Explorer.

Web Page—any single document displayed in the browser window.

Web pages may contain plain text, graphics, sounds, animation, hypertext links, and fill-in forms.

World Wide Web—one service made possible by the Internet.

It is the multimedia portion of the Internet — a place where text, pictures, sound, and videos on an array of topics are accessible to computers around the world.

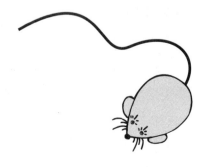

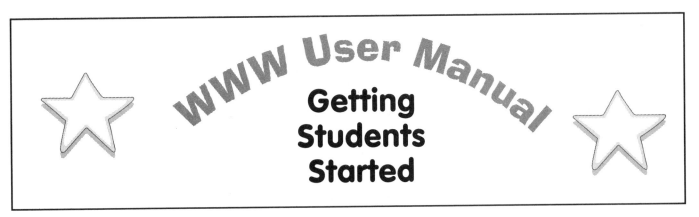

WWW User Manual

Getting Students Started

Introducing the Web as a Classroom Tool

Ask students where they would look for information if they wanted to learn about something. Write their responses on the chalkboard or a chart.

Where We Look for Information

books
magazines
grown-ups
television
parks
maps
encyclopedias

Sometimes I find the information in books!

If the computer or the World Wide Web is not mentioned, explain that you have a tool in your classroom that combines many of the resources that the class has listed. It is like a book, an encyclopedia, an atlas, a television news program, a field trip, and a magazine all in one. It is part of a computer network that connects people all over the world so that they can share information.

Make an overhead transparency of page 14 and use it to point out the special features of the World Wide Web and to talk about the importance of each feature.

Note: The fact that anyone can publish a Web page is both positive and negative. Use the discussion of this Web page feature to introduce evaluating resources.

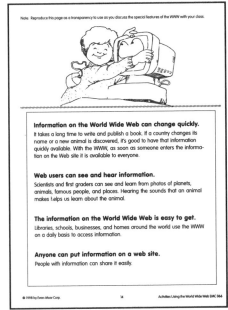

Note: Reproduce this page as a transparency to use as you discuss the special features of the WWW with your class.

Information on the World Wide Web can change quickly.
It takes a long time to write and publish a book. If a country changes its name or a new animal is discovered, it's good to have that information quickly available. With the WWW, as soon as someone enters the information on the Web site it is available to everyone.

Web users can see and hear information.
Scientists and first graders can see and learn from photos of planets, animals, famous people, and places. Hearing the sounds that an animal makes helps us learn about the animal.

The information on the World Wide Web is easy to get.
Libraries, schools, businesses, and homes around the world use the WWW on a daily basis to access information.

Anyone can put information on a web site.
People with information can share it easily.

© 1998 by Evan-Moor Corp.　　14　　Activities Using the World Wide Web EMC 066

Information on the World Wide Web can change quickly.

It takes a long time to write and publish a book. If a country changes its name or a new animal is discovered, it's good to have that information quickly available. With the WWW, as soon as someone enters the information on the Web site it is available to everyone.

Web users can see and hear information.

Scientists and first graders can see and learn from photos of planets, animals, famous people, and places. Hearing the sounds that an animal makes helps us learn about the animal.

The information on the World Wide Web is easy to get.

Libraries, schools, businesses, and homes around the world use the WWW on a daily basis to access information.

Anyone can put information on a web site.

People with information can share it easily.

Talking with Your Students about Evaluating Web Sites

Here is one way you might explain the need for looking carefully at a source of information before accepting it as valid.

Before the Demonstration

- Bookmark the *Dole Five-a-Day Learning about Apples* site (from the lesson on page 18) on the computer that you will use for the demonstration.

  (http://www.dole5aday.com/about/apple/apple.html#table)

- Hook the computer monitor to your classroom television with a video-out cable so that students can see more easily.

- Reproduce a copy of the simple evaluation checklist found on page 59 to use in the demonstration.

The Demonstration

1 Say:

If a carpenter is building a house, the carpenter will use a good hammer and good wood so that the house will be strong. If a scientist is solving an important problem, the scientist uses accurate information and calculations so that the answer will be correct. If second graders are learning about African animals, the second graders need good facts so that the information they learn is true.

Every time we use any source of information, we must decide whether it's good information. Each time we visit a Web site, we will look at it carefully to see if the information is accurate, up-to-date, and understandable. We can use this simple checklist to record our evaluation. (Show the evaluation form.)

Suppose that we needed some information about different varieties of apples. Let's look at one web site that I bookmarked and evaluate the site to see if we should use it.

2

Open the Internet connection.

Open the Learning about Apples bookmark.

I'll write the name of the site on the checklist. Write Learning about Apples.

Explain:

When I found the Apples site, I liked the way it looked. There were good pictures of the apples and not too much print. This format makes the page understandable. I'll circle "yes" after "Is the information understandable?"

3

Scroll to the bottom of the page.

I looked at the bottom of the page to see who wrote the information. The apple page is sponsored by the Dole Food Company as part of their Five-a-Day education program. They got the apple information from the Washington State Apple Commission. Both of these groups are good sources. I'll write the two sources on the blank where it asks who created the Web site. I think that the information is good, so I'll circle "yes" after "Is the information good?" Now I need to know whether the page is up-to-date.

Point out the date of copyright and revision.

The page was last revised just three months ago, so the information is up-to-date. I can circle "yes" after "Is the information up-to-date?"

4

I circled "yes" in each area of my checklist, so I want to remember where this site is and access it quickly.

Show how a bookmark is made.

I bookmarked this site for us to use. Now whenever we need to use the Learning about Apples site we will go to bookmarks, scroll down to Learning about Apples, and we'll be ready to learn about different varieties of apples.

 Activities Using the World Wide Web EMC 066

Navigating a Web Page

Once you have found a Web site that has the information that you are looking for, you will need to move through that Web site. Here are some of the ways that you can move through a Web site. Demonstrate each technique for your students as you do the whole class activities in this book.

Scrolling Down

A text box with an arrow on the right side tells you that there is more text than will fit in the box. You will need to scroll down to see it all. Press on the arrow pointing down at the bottom of the bar and the text will come into view.

Expanding the Browser Window

To make the Web site window fill the screen of the monitor, click on the resize box (Maximize button) in the upper right-hand corner.

Hyperlinks

The blue or purple words on the screen *link* to other documents. Just click on the words. Blue words turn purple when they have been accessed. The new documents may be in the same web location or a completely different site.

Note: Although hyperlinks are traditionally blue, other colors are possible. When searching for links, look for other colors as well.

Using Bookmarks

A bookmark is a way to mark a site that you've already visited so that you can go there quickly without having to type the site's URL. Open your Web browser, pull down the bookmark file (favorites file) and highlight the site you want. Hotlist is another name for a collection of bookmarks.

Pop-up Menu

In addition to the pull-down menus at the top of the screen, both Netscape Navigator and Internet Explorer provide pop-up menus containing navigational choices. To display the pop-up menu, position the mouse over a clickable element and click the right button (PC) or hold the mouse button down (MAC).

Back Key

A great thing about the WWW is that you can't get lost. Just click on the Back key on the tool bar at the top of the screen to go back one page. Keep clicking to get back to where you started.

Copying an Image (Copy and Paste)

For a MAC
Press the mouse button while the cursor hand is on the image that you want to copy. A pop-up menu will appear. Choose "Copy the Image" from the menu. (This puts the image on the computer clipboard.) Then you move to the document where the image will be used and paste it in place.

Note: You must bring the image into your program as a graphic object. Check to make sure you have the right tool before pasting the image.

For a PC
Move the cursor over the image you want to copy. Click the right button on your mouse to see the pop-up menu. Choose "Copy" from the menu. (This puts the image on the computer clipboard.). Move to the document where the image will be used and paste it in place.

Hide a Program

To keep one program open and open another, you can go to the application menu or bar and choose "Hide" (Mac) or "Minimize" (PC). Now you can open the new program. When you want the first program to open on the screen again, either go to the application menu and choose the name of the program (Mac), or click on the program name on the task bar (PC).

Work between Two Programs

If you are cutting and pasting information or graphics from one program to another, you may want to keep both programs (applications) open on the desktop at the same time. Use the application menu to choose the one you want to see.

Learning about Apples

In this set of lessons, students will review thirteen different varieties of apples as a whole class, graph apple attributes in small groups, and individually create a page describing a new apple.

Different Kinds of Apples

A Whole Class Project

http://www.dole5aday.com/menu/educators/menu.html

This site is a commercial Web site sponsored by Dole Food Company. They have developed the site as a part of their education program. It is an excellent site for discovering basic information about different varieties of apples.

Before the Activity

1. Open the Internet connection.

2. Enter the URL in the location field.

3. Press "Return" to open the site.
   (You are loading the site into your computer's cache so that it will be more quickly accessed when you are working with the class.)

4. Add a bookmark (favorite) for the site. Name it Cool Stuff about Apples (This makes it possible to return to the location without entering the complete URL each time.)

The Activity

1. Open the Internet connection.

2. Open the bookmark for the Dole *Cool Stuff about Apples* site.

3. Model evaluating the site. (See the modeling sample on page 15.) Help students determine that it is a commercial site with objective, up-to-date information.

4. Scroll through the row of apples. Read the names. Look at each different apple.

5. Click on a name. Read the information about that specific apple variety.

6. Repeat for a different apple.

> This is a good time to try several of the apple varieties that you are reading about.
> - Taste the apples.
> - Reread the captions.
> - Think of new words and phrases that describe how you feel about the apples.

Graphing Apple Attributes

A Small Group Activity

Before the Activity

1. Reproduce and post the *Graphing Apple Attributes* student directions on page 20.

2. Reproduce the *Learning about Apples* notetaker (page 60) and *Apple Attribute Graph* (page 61) for each group.

3. As a demonstration, open the bookmarked *Cool Stuff about Apples* site. Click on an apple. Model the process of reading a caption, locating a keyword, and recording it on the notetaker.

4. Divide your class into small groups.

5. For beginning readers, have cross-age tutors or parent helpers available for reading.

> Note: Be sure to give helpers or tutors some basic instruction about their role in the project. Their main function is to read information to the group of students. Students should be responsible for listening for and identifying keywords. The helper or tutor might record the information on a group notetaker or individuals can record information themselves.

The Activity

1. Open the Internet connection.

2. Open the *Cool Stuff about Apples* bookmark.

3. Read about eight different apples. As you read, write on the notetaker the name of each apple and keywords that tell about it.

4. Make a graph that shows the information you gathered.

   - Choose three attributes from your notetaker that several apples share.

   - Write the attributes under the rows on the graph.

   - Color in the squares to show how many of the apples have each attribute.

   - Give your graph a title.

   (If your students are familiar with a graphing program on the computer, use the program to create the graph.)

Page 20

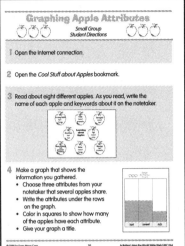

Page 60

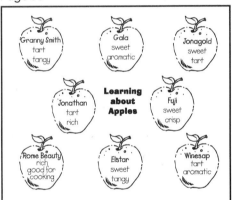

Page 61

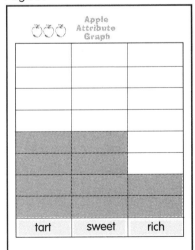

Graphing Apple Attributes

Small Group
Student Directions

1 Open the Internet connection.

2 Open the *Cool Stuff about Apples* bookmark.

3 Read about eight different apples. As you read, write the name of each apple and keywords about it on the notetaker.

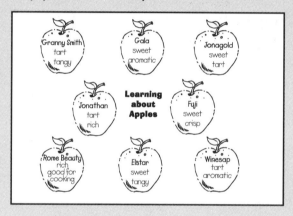

4 Make a graph that shows the information you gathered.
- Choose three attributes from your notetaker that several apples share.
- Write the attributes under the rows on the graph.
- Color in squares to show how many of the apples have each attribute.
- Give your graph a title.

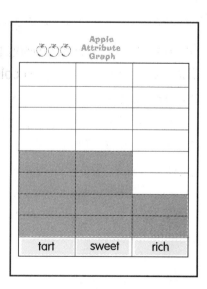

My Very Own Apple

An Individual Project

Before the Activity

1. Decide whether students will use computer drawing tools or traditional drawing tools to create their apple posters. Student directions for completing the project using computer drawing tools are included on page 22. Reproduce the student directions and post them beside the computer(s) that will be used.

2. Have students brainstorm words that are used to describe apples. Record the words in an apples' word bank and post it beside the computer.

The Activity—Reading about My Favorite Apple

1. Open the Internet connection.

2. Open the bookmark for *Cool Stuff about Apples.*

3. Click on your favorite apple. Look at the page. Notice the picture, the name, and the words.

4. Think about a new kind of apple.

   What would it look like?

   What would it taste like?

   How would you tell about it?

   What would you name it?

5. Quit the Internet connection.

Page 22

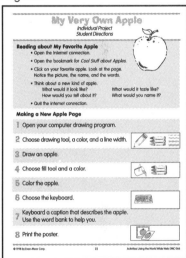

The Activity—Making a New Apple Page

1. Open your computer drawing program.

2. Choose the drawing tool, a color, and a line width.

3. Draw an apple.

4. Choose the fill tool and a color.

5. Color the apple.

6. Choose the keyboard.

7. Keyboard a caption that describes the apple. Use the word bank to help you.

8. Print the poster.

Amy's Amazing Apple

Amy's Amazing Apple tastes sweet when it is baked. Its pink skin is tart.

My Very Own Apple

Individual Project
Student Directions

Reading about My Favorite Apple

- Open the Internet connection.

- Open the bookmark for *Cool Stuff about Apples.*

- Click on your favorite apple. Look at the page.
  Notice the picture, the name, and the words.

- Think about a new kind of apple.
  - What would it look like? What would it taste like?
  - How would you tell about it? What would you name it?

- Quit the Internet connection.

Making a New Apple Page

1 Open your computer drawing program.

2 Choose the drawing tool, a color, and a line width.

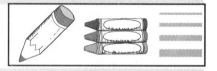

3 Draw an apple.

4 Choose the fill tool and a color.

5 Color the apple.

6 Choose the keyboard.

7 Keyboard a caption that describes the apple. Use the word bank to help you.

8 Print the poster.

Learning about the Planets

In this set of lessons, students will explore the Solar System as a whole class, research one of the planets in a small group, and then individually create a picture postcard describing their "travels" in space.

The Solar System

A Whole Class Project

http://www.tcsn.net/afiner/intro.htm (Nine Planets Just for Kids)

Optional Sites:

http://seds.lpl.arizona.edu/nineplanets/nineplanets.html#toc

http://www.hawastsoc.org/solar/

http://stardate.utexas.edu/resources/ssguide/ssg_contents.html

http://pds/jpl.nasa.gov/planets/welcome.htm

Each of the sites listed above is an informational site sponsored by a University or by NASA. They are excellent sites with valuable and accurate information.

Note: The amount of information presented can be overwhelming. For beginning readers, have cross-age tutors or parent helpers available for reading. The photographs and drawings are excellent.

Before the Activity

1. Open the Internet connection.
2. Enter a URL in the location field.
3. Press "Return" to open the site.
4. Look at each of the sites and determine which one best fits the needs of your class.

   (The following activity is designed using the *Nine Planets Just for Kids* site.)
5. Bookmark the location that you will use.
6. Practice your tour of the solar system.

The Activity

1. Using the bookmark, open the *Nine Planets Just for Kids* site.
2. Use the scroll bar at the right of the page to move through the page. Read the text together and note the links to other pages.
3. At the bottom of the page, click on the rocket to move to a page that compares the nine planets. Enjoy the comparison.
4. When the tour is finished, have students define "solar system." Record their definition on the chalkboard, a chart, or a computer document.
5. Make a list of the elements of the solar system — the sun, the nine planets, the asteroid belt.

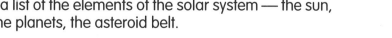

Visiting a Planet

A Small Group Project

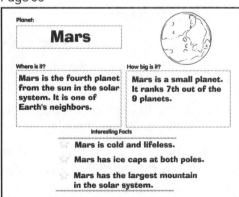

Before the Activity

1. Reproduce the planet research notetaker (page 62) for each group.

2. Scan the template on page 63 and save it as *Planet Report* on the computer(s) to be used.

3. For beginning readers, have cross-age tutors or parent helpers available for reading.

   Note: Be sure to give helpers or tutors some basic instruction about their role in the project. Their main function is to read information to the group of students. Students should be responsible for listening for and identifying keywords. The tutor or helper might record the information on a group notetaker, or individuals can record information themselves.

4. Assign planets or have groups choose their planets.

5. Model the process of reading information, locating answers to questions on the notetaker, and recording the information.

6. Demonstrate how an image is copied from the WWW site and pasted to the report. (See page 17 for directions.)

The Activity—On the World Wide Web

1. Open the Internet connection.

2. Open *The Nine Planets Just for Kids* bookmark.

3. Click on a planet's name in the text.

4. Read the information about the planet.

5. Using keywords, answer the questions on the notetaker.

6. Stop at the Planet Pit Stop and determine your weight on your planet.

7. Close the *Nine Planets Just for Kids* site.

Page 62

The Activity—Reporting Your Information

1. Open the *Planet Report* template.

2. Choose the keyboard.

3. Keyboard information to complete the report.

4. Hide the template.

5. Open the *Nine Planets Just for Kids* bookmark.

6. Find a picture of your planet.

7. Copy the image. Close the *Nine Planets Just for Kids* site.

8. Choose your template and paste the picture onto your report.

9. Print the report.

Page 63

Planet Report

On the World Wide Web

1. Open the Internet connection.
2. Open *The Nine Planets Just for Kids* bookmark.
3. Click on a planet's name in the text.
4. Read the information about the planet.
5. Using keywords, answer the questions on the notetaker.
6. Stop at the Planet Pit Stop and determine your weight on your planet.
7. Close the *Nine Planets Just for Kids* site.

Reporting Your Information

1 Open the *Planet Report* template.

2 Choose the keyboard.

3 Keyboard information to complete the report.

4 Hide the template.

5 Open the *Nine Planets Just for Kids* bookmark.

6 Find a picture of your planet.

7 Copy the image. Close the *Nine Planets Just for Kids* site.

8 Choose your template and paste the picture onto your report.

9 Print the report.

Postcard from a Planet

An Individual Project

Before the Activity

1. Scan the postcard template on page 64 onto the computer(s) that will be used.
2. Save the template as *Planet Postcard.*

The Activity

1. Think about what it would be like to actually visit the planet that you studied. What would you write home about?

2. Open the *Planet Postcard* template.

3. Choose the keyboard. Write a message as if you were sending a card home from the planet.

4. Hide (minimize) the template.

5. Open the Internet connection. Open the *Nine Planets Just for Kids* bookmark.

6. Find an image for the picture part of your postcard.

7. Copy the image.

8. Close or hide the Internet connection.

9. Open the *Planet Postcard* template.

10. Paste the image onto your postcard.

11. Turn the image upside down so that you can fold the postcard when it is printed.

12. Print the postcard.

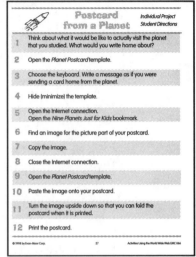

Page 27

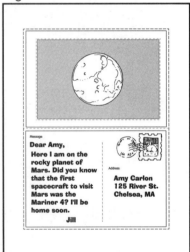

Page 64

Postcard from a Planet

1 Think about what it would be like to actually visit the planet that you studied. What would you write home about?

2 Open the *Planet Postcard* template.

3 Choose the keyboard. Write a message as if you were sending a card home from the planet.

4 Hide (minimize) the template.

5 Open the Internet connection.
Open the *Nine Planets Just for Kids* bookmark.

6 Find an image for the picture part of your postcard.

7 Copy the image.

8 Close the Internet connection.

9 Open the *Planet Postcard* template.

10 Paste the image onto your postcard.

11 Turn the image upside down so that you can fold the postcard when it is printed.

12 Print the postcard.

Learning about Animals

In this set of activities, the whole class will learn more about an animal; small groups of students will compare a mammal, a reptile, and an amphibian; and, finally, individual students will study one animal of their choice. The individual reports will be put together as a class resource.

Many Different Creatures

A Whole Class Project

http://www.seaworld.org./animal_bytes/animal_bytes.html

The *Animal Bytes* site is sponsored by Sea World. It was designed to help users quickly find information about specific animals. The information is accurate and current.

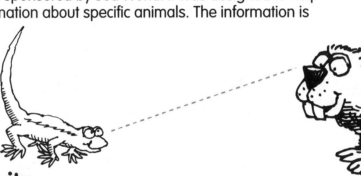

Before the Activity

1. Open the Internet connection.
2. Enter the URL in the location field.
3. Press "Return" to open the *Animal Bytes* site.
4. Bookmark the location (add to favorites).
5. Choose an animal for your research. You may want to choose an animal from a current unit of study, an animal from a book read aloud to the class, an animal in the news, or one that interests you. Check to make sure that the animal is included in the *Animal Bytes* site.
6. Make an overhead transparency of the KWL chart on page 65.

The Activity

1. Talk with the class about the animal you have chosen.
2. Fill in the "Know" and "Want to Know" sections on the overhead chart.
3. Open the *Animal Bytes* bookmark.
4. Click on the animal that you have chosen.
5. Read the information aloud.
6. Record keywords on the "Learned" section of the overhead chart.

A Mammal, a Reptile, and an Amphibian

A Small Group Project

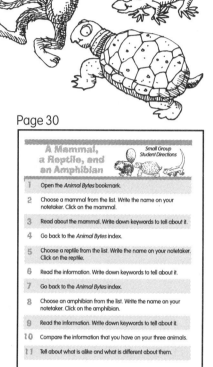

Before the Activity

1. Reproduce the *Mammal, Reptile, Amphibian* notetaker on page 66 for each group.

2. Reproduce and post *A Mammal, a Reptile, and an Amphibian* student directions on page 30.

3. Form small groups of three or four students.

4. Contact parent helpers or cross-age tutors.

> Note: Be sure to give helpers or tutors some basic instruction about their role in the project. Their main function is to read information to the group of students. Students should be responsible for listening for and identifying keywords. The helper might record the information on a group notetaker, or individuals can record information themselves.

The Activity

1. Open the *Animal Bytes* bookmark.

2. Choose a mammal from the list. Write the name on your notetaker. Click on the mammal.

3. Read about the mammal. Write down keywords to tell about it.

4. Go back to the *Animal Bytes* index.

5. Choose a reptile from the list. Write the name on your notetaker. Click on the reptile.

6. Read the information. Write down keywords to tell about it.

7. Go back to the *Animal Bytes* index.

8. Choose an amphibian from the list. Write the name on your notetaker. Click on the amphibian.

9. Read the information. Write down keywords to tell about it.

10. Compare the information on the three animals.

11. Tell about similarities and differences among them.

Page 30

A Mammal,
a Reptile, and
an Amphibian

Small Group Student Directions

1 Open the *Animal Bytes* bookmark.

2 Choose a mammal from the list. Write the name on your notetaker. Click on the mammal.

3 Read about the mammal. Write down keywords to tell about it.

4 Go back to the *Animal Bytes* index.

5 Choose a reptile from the list. Write the name on your notetaker. Click on the reptile.

6 Read the information. Write down keywords to tell about it.

7 Go back to the *Animal Bytes* index.

8 Choose an amphibian from the list. Write the name on your notetaker. Click on the amphibian.

9 Read the information. Write down keywords to tell about it.

10 Compare the information that you have on your three animals.

11 Tell about what is alike and what is different about them.

© 1998 by Evan-Moor Corp.   30   Activities Using the World Wide Web EMC 066

Page 66

	Mammal cinnamon bear	Amphibian bullfrog	Reptile sea turtle
Where it lives	mountains of North America	North America along edge of large, slow moving bodies of fresh water	tropical and temperate seas throughout the world
What it eats	insects, fruit, vegetables, honey, occasionally meat	anything that moves that it can swallow: mammals, birds, fish reptiles, turtles	varies among species: seagrass, algae, crabs, shrimp
What it looks like	males larger 3½ ft tall 3–7 ft long 200–500 pounds	flat, broad body and head green to greenish-brown	long, paddle-like flippers range in length from 21" to 6 ft
Interesting Facts	• smallest bear • excellent climber • good swimmer	• can leap 3–6 feet • lays up to 25,000 eggs • breathes through skin	• endangered species • hearts slow underwater • some can stay underwater for 5 hours

A Mammal, a Reptile, and an Amphibian

1 Open the *Animal Bytes* bookmark.

2 Choose a mammal from the list. Write the name on your notetaker. Click on the mammal.

3 Read about the mammal. Write down keywords to tell about it.

4 Go back to the *Animal Bytes* index.

5 Choose a reptile from the list. Write the name on your notetaker. Click on the reptile.

6 Read the information. Write down keywords to tell about it.

7 Go back to the *Animal Bytes* index.

8 Choose an amphibian from the list. Write the name on your notetaker. Click on the amphibian.

9 Read the information. Write down keywords to tell about it.

10 Compare the information that you have on your three animals.

11 Tell about what is alike and what is different about them.

Introducing the _____

An Individual Project

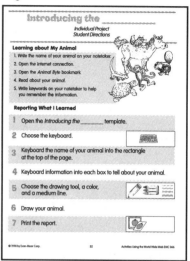

Page 32

Before the Activity

1. Have students choose an animal that they will introduce to the class.

2. Depending on the reading level of your students, you may want to have cross-age tutors or parent helpers available for reading the text during research periods.

   Note: Be sure to give helpers or tutors some basic instruction about their role in the project. Their main function is to read information to the group of students. Students should be responsible for listening for and identifying keywords. The helper might record the information on a group notetaker, or individuals can record information themselves.

3. Reproduce the notetaker on page 67 for each student.

4. Reproduce and post *Introducing the* _____ student directions on page 32.

5. Scan the template on page 68 and save it as *Introducing the*_____ on the computer(s) that students will use.

The Activity—Learning about My Animal

Page 67

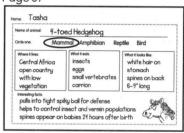

1. Write the name of your animal on your notetaker.

2. Open the Internet connection.

3. Open the *Animal Bytes* bookmark.

4. Read about your animal.

5. Write keywords on your notetaker to help you remember the information.

The Activity—Reporting What I Learned

Page 68

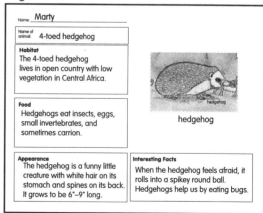

1. Open the *Introducing the*_____ template.

2. Choose the keyboard.

3. Keyboard the name of your animal into the rectangle at the top of the page.

4. Keyboard information into each box to tell about your animal.

5. Choose the drawing tool, a color, and a medium line.

6. Draw your animal.

7. Print the report.

After the Activity

Share student reports by binding the hard copies into a class book or making a computer slide show using the saved computer copies. (See page 6 for directions.)

Introducing the _____

Individual Project
Student Directions

Learning about My Animal

1. Write the name of your animal on your notetaker.

2. Open the Internet connection.

3. Open the *Animal Bytes* bookmark.

4. Read about your animal.

5. Write keywords on your notetaker to help you remember the information.

Reporting What I Learned

1 Open the *Introducing the _____* template.

2 Choose the keyboard.

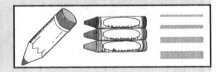

3 Keyboard the name of your animal into the rectangle at the top of the page.

4 Keyboard information into each box to tell about your animal.

5 Choose the drawing tool, a color, and a medium line.

6 Draw your animal.

7 Print the report.

Learning about the Fifty States

In this set of activities, students will explore the information contained in a state site and evaluate what is important to know about the state. The teacher will use this information to complete the notetaker which will then be used for the small group project. In small groups, they will find out about one state. As individuals, they will create a poster representing the state.

What's Important to Know?

A Whole Class Project

http://www.50states.com

This site is written and maintained by Ray Weber in Santa Clarita, California. It is a personal Web page but contains basic, objective, up-to-date information about the fifty states and links to many additional sites with more information.

Before the Activity

1. Open the Internet connection.

2. Enter the URL in the location field.

3. Press "Return" to open the *Fifty States* site.

4. Bookmark the site on your computer(s).

5. Make an overhead transparency of the notetaker on page 69.

The Activity

1. Open the Internet connection.

2. Using your bookmark (favorites) menu, open the *Fifty States* site.

3. Demonstrate the features:

   • Click on the small U.S. map labeled "State" to see a map of the United States with the states labeled.

   • Click on the small U.S. map labeled "Capital" to see a map with the states and capitals labeled.

   • Click on the folder labeled "Birds" for a list of the state birds.

   • Note that states are listed by postal code. Click on a state to review the information included for the state.

4. Talk about the types of information included. As a class, decide on four things that are most important to know about a state. For example: capital, population, size, etc.

5. Write the four things in the heading spaces on your copy of the notetaker.

Looking at One State

A Small Group Project

Before the Activity

Page 35

1. Make a copy of the notetaker on page 69. Fill in the four important things to know that you wrote on the overhead (page 33). Reproduce the notetaker for each student.

2. Form small groups of three or four students.

3. Have each group choose a state or assign one to each group.

4. Contact parent helpers or cross-age tutors for reading assistance if necessary.

Note: Be sure to give helpers or tutors some basic instruction about their role in the project. Their main function is to read information to the group of students. Students should be responsible for listening for and identifying keywords. The helper might record the information on a group notetaker, or individuals can record information themselves.

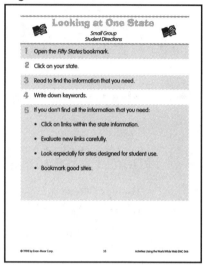

The Activity

1. Open the *Fifty States* bookmark.

2. Click on your state.

3. Read to find the information that you need.

4. Write down keywords.

5. If you don't find all the information that you need:

   • Click on links within the state information.

   • Evaluate new links carefully.

   • Look especially for sites designed for student use. (such as Colorado's home page addition—*Especially for Kids* http://www.state.co.us/kids/index.html)

   • Bookmark good sites.

Page 69

Name: Dianna R.	Name of state: Colorado
Border States	**State Flag**
Arizona Oklahoma Kansas Utah Nebraska Wyoming New Mexico	3 alternate stripes adopted in 1911 C
Name and Nickname	**Capital**
origin in Spanish "colored red" name chosen by Congress Centennial State Colorful Colorado	Denver also largest city

Looking at One State

Small Group
Student Directions

1 Open the *Fifty States* bookmark.

2 Click on your state.

3 Read to find the information that you need.

4 Write down keywords.

5 If you don't find all the information that you need:

- Click on links within the state information.

- Evaluate new links carefully.

- Look especially for sites designed for student use.

- Bookmark good sites.

A State Poster Presentation

An Individual Project

Before the activity

1. Reproduce the template on page 70 for each student or scan it onto the computer(s).
2. Save it as *State Poster*. (The directions below are for designing the poster using the computer template.)

The Activity

1. Open the *State Poster* template.
2. Choose the keyboard.
3. Keyboard the name of your state into the center rectangle.
4. Look at each section of your notetaker.
5. Use the keywords to help you write a sentence for each heading on your notetaker.
6. Keyboard the sentences into the rectangles on the *State Poster* template.
7. Choose the fill tool and a color.
8. Fill each of the rectangles with color.
9. Choose the drawing tools, a color, and a line width.
10. Draw pictures to tell more about your state.
11. Choose the fill tool to color the pictures.

After the Activity

Use the individual poster presentations as part of a slide show (see page 6 for directions on making one) or print the posters and display them with the notetakers.

Page 37

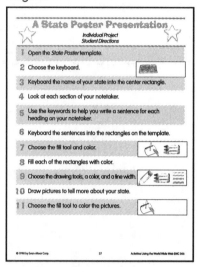

Page 70

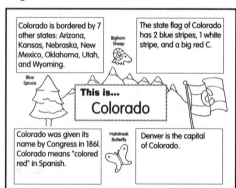

A State Poster Presentation

Individual Project
Student Directions

1 Open the *State Poster* template.

2 Choose the keyboard.

3 Keyboard the name of your state into the center rectangle.

4 Look at each section of your notetaker.

5 Use the keywords to help you write a sentence for each heading on your notetaker.

6 Keyboard the sentences into the rectangles on the template.

7 Choose the fill tool and a color.

8 Fill each of the rectangles with color.

9 Choose the drawing tools, a color, and a line width.

10 Draw pictures to tell more about your state.

11 Choose the fill tool to color the pictures.

Learning about the White House

In this set of lessons, students will visit the *White House for Kids* site. As a class, they will learn about the history of the White House. In small groups, they will look at different rooms in the White House. As individuals, they will read about children who have lived in the White House and then write about what they think it would be like to live there.

A Famous House

A Whole Class Project

http://www.whitehouse.gov/WH/kids/html/kidshome.html

This kid-friendly site is sponsored by the Office of the President and is maintained by its Web Development Team. It includes links to additional information on the White House for more in-depth research.

Before the Activity

1. Open the Internet connection.

2. Enter the URL in the location field.

3. Press "Return" to open *The White House for Kids* site.

4. Bookmark the site on your computer(s).

5. Reproduce the time line on page 71 for each student and make a transparency on which to take class notes.

The Activity

1. Open the Internet connection.

2. Open *The White House for Kids* bookmark.

3. Click to read the sign that says *Come Visit the White House for Kids*.

4. Choose 1 from the menu to read about where the White House is located. (Check your own world and U.S. maps. Locate the District of Columbia.) Then use the Web map to locate the White House.

5. Click on 2 to read about the history of the White House. Read as much information as is appropriate for your students.

6. Teacher writes keywords on the time line transparency.

7. Students use the keywords to complete individual time lines.

Touring the White House

A Small Group Project

Page 40

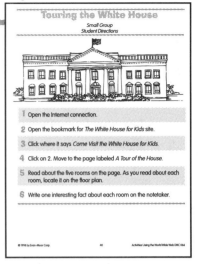

Before the Activity

1. Reproduce and post the *Touring the White House* student directions on page 40.

2. Reproduce the *White House Floor Plan* map on page 72 and the *White House Floor Plan* notetaker on page 73 for each student.

3. Divide the class into small groups.

4. Contact parent helpers or cross-age tutors if necessary for reading assistance.

Note: Be sure to give helpers or tutors some basic instruction about their role in the project. Their main function is to read information to the group of students. Students should be responsible for listening for and identifying keywords. The helper might record the information on a group notetaker, or individuals can record information themselves.

Page 72

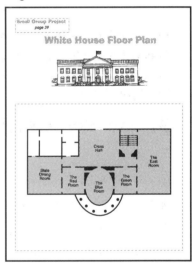

The Activity

1. Open the Internet connection.

2. Open the bookmark for *The White House for Kids* site.

3. Click where it says *Come Visit the White House for Kids.*

4. Click on 2. Move to the page labeled *A Tour of the House.*

5. Read about the five rooms on the page. As you read about each room, locate it on the floor plan.

6. Write one interesting fact about each room in the correct notetaker box.

Page 73

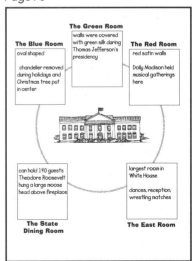

Touring the White House

1 Open the Internet connection.

2 Open the bookmark for *The White House for Kids* site.

3 Click where it says *Come Visit the White House for Kids*.

4 Click on 2. Move to the page labeled *A Tour of the House*.

5 Read about the five rooms on the page. As you read about each room, locate it on the floor plan.

6 Write one interesting fact about each room on the notetaker.

Activities Using the World Wide Web EMC 066

Living in the White House

An Individual Project

Before the Activity

1. Reproduce the *Living in the White House* template on page 74 for each student or scan it onto the computer(s) that will be used. The directions below are for using the computer template.

2. Save it as *White House.*

The Activity

1. Open the Internet connection.

2. Open *The White House For Kids* bookmark.

3. Click on *Come Visit the White House for Kids.*
   Click on *4 — Children of the White House.*

4. Look at the children who have lived in the White House. Read about what they did and how they felt. Think about how you would feel.

5. Close the Internet connection.

6. Open the *White House* template.

7. Choose the keyboard.

8. Keyboard to tell about what you think it would be like to live in the White House.

9. Choose the drawing tool, a color, and a line width.

10. Draw yourself outside the White House.

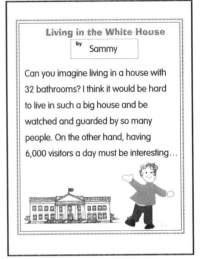

Page 74

Living in the White House

by Sammy

Can you imagine living in a house with 32 bathrooms? I think it would be hard to live in such a big house and be watched and guarded by so many people. On the other hand, having 6,000 visitors a day must be interesting…

Living in the White House

Individual Project
Student Directions

1 Open the Internet connection.

2 Open *The White House For Kids* bookmark.

3 Click on *Come Visit the White House for Kids.* Click on 4 — *Children of the White House.*

4 Look at the children who have lived in the White House. Read about what they did and how they felt. Think about how you would feel.

5 Close the Internet connection.

6 Open the *White House* template.

7 Choose the keyboard.

8 Keyboard to tell about what you think it would be like to live in the White House.

9 Choose the drawing tool, a color, and a line width.

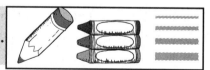

10 Draw yourself outside the White House.

Learning about Native Americans

In this set of activities, students will note the different locations of Native American tribes on a map of the United States, choose a tribe to learn more about, and complete an individual report on that tribe.

Discovering Diversity

A Whole Class Project

http://www.ilt.columbia.edu/k12/naha/maps/nausa.html

Using a map from the Smithsonian Institution, this site instructs you to click on areas of the map labeled with Native American Tribes. You zoom in on the precise area and the tribes of that region. The site links to the *Native American Navigator* which in turn links to information on specific tribes. The site is sponsored by the Institute for Learning Technologies at Columbia University.

Before the Activity

1. Open the Internet connection.
2. Enter the URL in the location field.
3. Press "Return" to open the site.
4. Bookmark the location.
5. Reproduce the *Native American Map* notetaker on page 75 as a transparency.

The Activity

1. Open the Internet connection.
2. Open the *Native American Map* bookmark.
3. Have students identify the map of the United States.
4. Click on one of the colored regions on the map to zoom in to see the Native American tribes that live(d) there.
5. Write the names of the tribes on the transparency map.
6. Zoom in on several different regions to see the names of different tribes.
7. Click on one tribal name to zoom in further on specific information about the tribe.
8. Evaluate the site.
9. Write keywords on the notetaker.

One Native American Tribe

A Small Group Activity

Some examples of World Wide Web sites sponsored by Native American tribes include:

- Navajo — http://waltonfeed.com/peoples/navajo/culture.html
- Mohicans — http://unr.edu/homepage/shubinsk/mohican1.html
- Makah — http://www.northolympic.com/makah/
- Ho-Chunk — http://www.ho-chunk.com/HISTORY.htm
- Cree — http://www.lib.uconn.edu/ArcticCircle/CulturalViability/Cree/creereserve.html
  http://www.ouje.ca/welcome/chief.htm
- Cherokee — http://www.powersource.com/powersource/nation/default.html
- Cheyenne and Arapaho — http://www.cheyenneandarapaho.org/indexframe.html

If you need additional information about any specific nation try this site:

http://www.pitt.edu/~lmitten/nations.html

The Web page, written and maintained by a librarian at the University of Pittsburgh, is a list of links to home pages of individual Native American nations.

Before the Activity

1. Bookmark the sites you wish your students to use. You might assign a particular tribe to only one group or to several groups.

2. Divide students into small groups.

3. Assign a Native American tribe to each group of students.

4. Reproduce the Native American notetaker (page 76) for each student.

5. You may want to arrange for parent helpers or cross-age tutors to help read the information.

Note: Be sure to give helpers or tutors some basic instruction about their role in the project. Their main function is to read information to the group of students. Students should be responsible for listening for and identifying keywords. The helper might record the information on a group notetaker, or individuals can record information themselves.

The Activity

1. Open the Internet connection.

2. Open the site bookmarked for your tribe.

3. Read the information.

4. Record keywords on your notetaker.

5. If you need more information on your tribe, follow links to related sites.

Page 45

Page 76

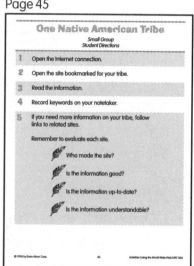

One Native American Tribe

1 Open the Internet connection.

2 Open the site bookmarked for your tribe.

3 Read the information.

4 Record keywords on your notetaker.

5 If you need more information on your tribe, follow links to related sites.

Remember to evaluate each site.

 Who made the site?

 Is the information good?

 Is the information up-to-date?

 Is the information understandable?

The Important Thing

An Individual Project

Before the Activity

1. Reproduce the template on page 77 for each student or scan the template into the computer(s) to be used, saving it as *Important Thing*.

2. Read Margaret Wise Brown's *The Important Book* (HarperCollins, 1949) so that students are familiar with the format they will be following.

3. Students will need the notetakers that were filled out in the small group activity (page 44).

The Activity

1. Read your notes on your Native American tribe.

2. Choose the piece of information you consider most important.

3. Open the *Important Thing* template.

4. Choose the keyboard.

5. Keyboard the name of the Native American tribe into the box at the top of the page.

6. Move to the long box. Keyboard: The most important thing about the (name of your tribe) tribe is _____. Finish the sentence with your idea.

7. Keyboard another fact by each feather.

8. Move to the box at the bottom of the page. Keyboard: But the most important thing about the (name of your tribe) tribe is _____.

    Be sure to repeat the idea you used in the first long box.

9. Hide (minimize) the template.

10. Open the Internet connection. Open your bookmarked site.

11. Copy an image. Quit the site.

12. Open your template. Paste the image to your report.

Page 47

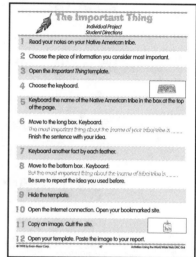

Page 77

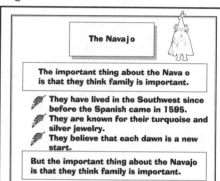

The Important Thing

1 Read your notes on your Native American tribe.

2 Choose the piece of information you consider most important.

3 Open the *Important Thing* template.

4 Choose the keyboard.

5 Keyboard the name of the Native American tribe into the box at the top of the page.

6 Move to the long box. Keyboard:
The most important thing about the *(name of your tribe)* tribe is _____.
Finish the sentence with your idea.

7 Keyboard another fact by each feather.

8 Move to the bottom box. Keyboard:
But the most important thing about the *(name of tribe)* tribe is _____.
Be sure to repeat the idea you used before.

9 Hide the template.

10 Open the Internet connection. Open your bookmarked site.

11 Copy an image. Quit the site.

12 Open your template. Paste the image to your report.

Web Searches
Effective Search Strategies

subject directory

key search

Two Ways to Search

At first, students will use World Wide Web sites that you have bookmarked for them. They will not be searching on their own. As they become more skilled, they can begin searching for information on their own. When they do, they will use one of two approaches for finding information on the Internet.

- The first is to use a **subject directory**. Students are presented with a list of very general subjects by a search engine. Choosing one of these subjects takes the student to another, more specific, list where another choice can be made to narrow the search. The process continues until specific Web page links are given. If you are interested in browsing general information, use a subject index instead of a keyword search.

- The quickest and most powerful way to find information on the Internet is to use a **keyword search**. Using a search engine, you look through a comprehensive database for a specific topic. You enter into a box keywords that represent a topic on the search engine home page. (The search is much like one you would do with the computerized card catalog at a library.) The search engine looks in a giant databank for web sites that reference your topic. The result is a list of links containing the terms you entered. Web search engines construct and retrieve information from databases of links to all kinds of information.

The lessons on pages 51 and 53 will help you to model the use of these two approaches for your students. Model each of the approaches several times, as well as the evaluation of the sites that you find, before your students search independently. Forms for tracking the results of these modeled searches are included on pages 52 and 54.

Pages 55–58 contain student directions and open-ended search maps for students to use when they begin independent searches. Post directions by the computer(s) for student reference. Reproduce the search maps and make them available near the computers.

Don't Forget Evaluation of New Sites

As capable students begin navigating and searching on their own, they will need to evaluate sites for themselves. A simplified checklist is provided on page 59. Model its use and then provide copies for students to use when they visit new sites.

Patience, Persistence, and Resourcefulness

You will need to be flexible in your search strategies and in your expectations in order to find useful information with a minimum of frustration.

- Give your modem and your computer time to retrieve the information that you have found.

- Know the requirements of the search engine you are using to structure your query correctly. Check on the help section for instructions specific to the search engine that you are using.

- Try different terms or different search engines until you find the results you want.

A wealth of resources is available on the Web. Help your students to be patient, persistent, and resourceful as they search.

See page 50 for a poster to put up to remind students of these valuable search traits.

When You're Searching...

Be Patient.
Let things happen.
Be Persistent.
Don't get discouraged.
Be Resourceful.
Be flexible. Try other words.

 Activities Using the World Wide Web EMC 066

Model a Subject Directory Search

A subject directory is helpful when you are searching for general information on a topic.

Below is a sample scenario that models the use of a subject directory.

You will need to log on to your Internet connection before beginning. You may want to hook your computer monitor to your classroom television with a video-out cable so that students can see more easily.

Make a transparency of the search map on page 52 to track your search. As you proceed, explain what you are doing and verbalize your thinking for students:

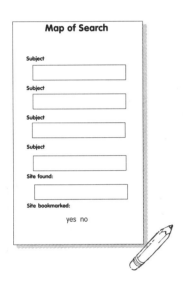

I want to find some information about whales. I have my search map, and I am ready to bookmark any sites where I can find the kind of information I'm going to need.

1. *I'll go to a search engine. I will use Yahoo for my search.*

2. *I'll read the list of subjects. What topic might include information about whales?*

3. *Science might, so I'll click on Science. I'll enter* **science** *on my tracking sheet.*

4. *I'll read the next, more specific list.*

5. *I'm going to try biology. I'll click on it. (Enter* **biology** *on the tracking sheet.)*

6. *I'll read the next list and choose marine biology. (Add* **marine biology** *to the tracking sheet.)*

7. *Finally, I click on whales. (Add* **whales** *to the tracking sheet.)*

8. *Here are some sites with information about whales. I'll read the descriptions and find one I like. Here's one called Whales that looks good. I'll click on it.*

9. *It's just a description of a film by National Geographic. I'll click on BACK to go back to the list of whale sites.*

10. *Here's one called Giants of the Deep by Lawrence Hall of Science. I know that LHS is part of the University of California at Berkeley so they should know what they're talking about. This describes an exhibit that they have. Look, we can listen to whale sounds. But this still isn't what I'm looking for. I'll click BACK to go back to the list again.*

11. *Here's one called* **Whale Times**. *Let's click on it. It has a section called Fishin' for Facts. I wonder who is responsible for this page? It looks like a personal Web page, but it has won several awards. Let's check out the facts and see if they seem to be accurate and up-to-date. The copyright says 1995. Here's a chart on specific whales. I'll click on the gray whale. This is good information, and I can understand it. I'm going to bookmark this site so I can come back to it. I'll add the URL to the bottom of my tracking sheet.*

 Activities Using the World Wide Web EMC 066

Note: Make a transparency of this search map to use with the lesson modeling a subject directory search (page 51).

Map of Search

Subject

Subject

Subject

Subject

Site found:

Site bookmarked:

yes no

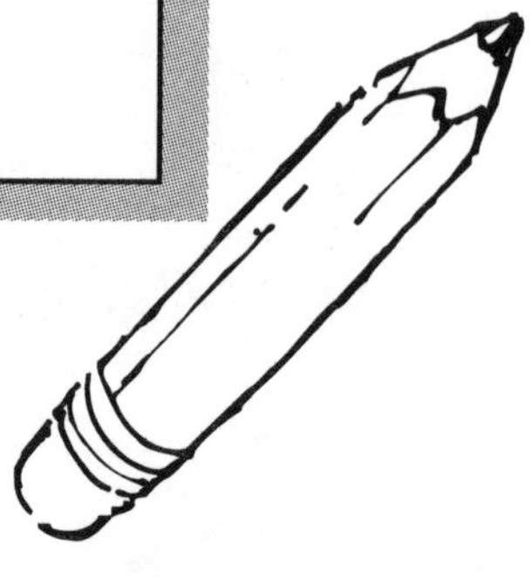

Model a Keyword Search

A keyword search helps you to find specific information more quickly than a subject directory search.

Here is a sample scenario for a model lesson on using a keyword search.

You will need to log on to your Internet connection before beginning. You may want to hook your computer monitor to your classroom television with a video-out cable so that students can see more easily. Make a transparency of the search map on page 54 to track your search.

As you proceed, explain what you are doing and verbalize your thinking for students:

I want to find some information about baleen whales. I have my search map, and I am ready to bookmark any sites where I can find the kind of information I'm going to need.

Let's find some information on baleen whales.

1. *I go to a search engine by clicking Search on the menu bar.*

2. *Next, I'll click my cursor in the blank box and keyboard in* **baleen whale** *and click on "Search." My results will be returned with the site that the search engine thinks is best, listed first.*

3. *I'll click on the first one. It's a WebQuest — that's a computer activity that we could do as a class. It doesn't have any information here.*

4. *I'll click on "Back" to go back to the list and try the next site. It's a Sea World site all about baleen whales. The scientists at Sea World would have good information for me.*

5. *Let's look at some of the information to make sure that it's easy to find and that we can understand it. I'll click on physical characteristics. Wow! It has lots of information. It tells about size, color, flippers, fins, flukes, heads, and lots more.*

6. *I'm going to bookmark this site so I can find it next time. Let's record some of the information on the search map.*

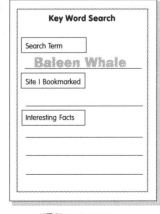

Note: Make a transparency of this search map to use with the lesson modeling a keyword search (page 53).

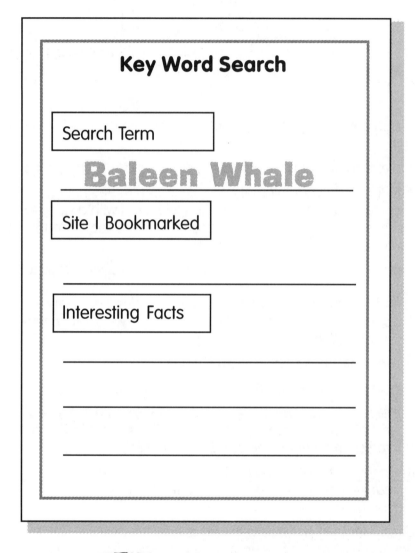

Key Word Search

Search Term

Baleen Whale

Site I Bookmarked

_____

Interesting Facts

_____

_____

_____

54   Activities Using the World Wide Web EMC 066

Doing a Subject Directory Search

When you are searching for general information on a topic, use these steps:

1. Go to a search engine.

2. Read the list of subjects.

3. Click on the one you want.

4. Read the next list.

5. Click on the one you want.

6. Repeat until you find the topic you want.

7. Click on the topic.

8. Evaluate the linked sites.

9. Bookmark the sites that you think will be helpful.

Map of Search

Subject:

Subject:

Subject:

Subject:

Subject:

Site found:

Site bookmarked:

yes   no

Computer #:

Map of Search

Subject:

Subject:

Subject:

Subject:

Subject:

Site found:

Site bookmarked:

yes   no

Computer #:

Doing a Keyword Search

When you are searching for specific information, follow these steps:

1. Go to a search engine.

2. Keyboard your search terms into the blank next to the word search.

3. Click on "Search" or press "Return."

4. Read the results.

5. Choose and visit sites.

6. Evaluate the sites.

7. Bookmark the sites that you think will be helpful.

Key Word Search

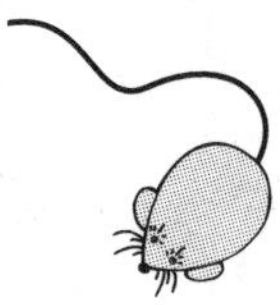

Search Terms

____

Site I Bookmarked

____

Interesting Facts

____

____

____

Key Word Search

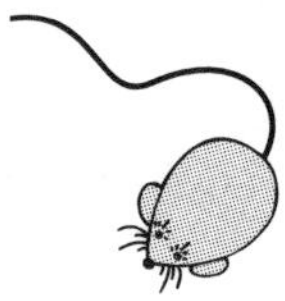

Search Terms

Site I Bookmarked

Interesting Facts

© 1998 by Evan-Moor Corp.

Key Word Search

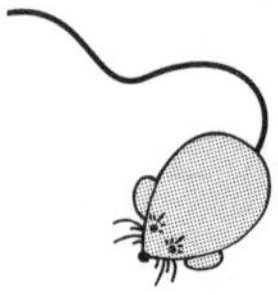

Search Terms

Site I Bookmarked

Interesting Facts

© 1998 by Evan-Moor Corp.

Key Word Search

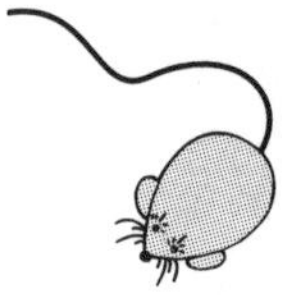

Search Terms

Site I Bookmarked

Interesting Facts

© 1998 by Evan-Moor Corp.

Simple Evaluation Checklist

URL of the Web site:

Who made the Web site?

Is the information good?   yes   no

Is the information up-to-date?   yes   no

Is the information understandable?   yes   no

This | is   is not | a good place to get information.

- -

Simple Evaluation Checklist

URL of the Web site:

Who made the Web site?

Is the information good?   yes   no

Is the information up-to-date?   yes   no

Is the information understandable?   yes   no

This | is   is not | a good place to get information.

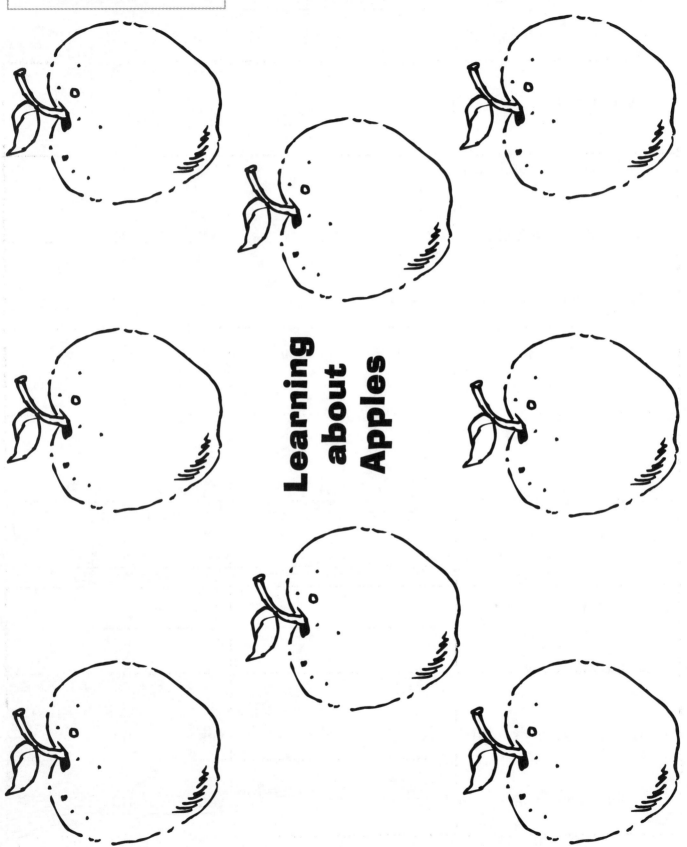

Learning about Apples

Apple Attribute Graph

Activities Using the World Wide Web EMC 066

Small Group Project

page 24

Name of Planet:

Where is it?

How big is it?

Interesting Facts:

Planet:

How big is it?

Where is it?

Interesting Facts

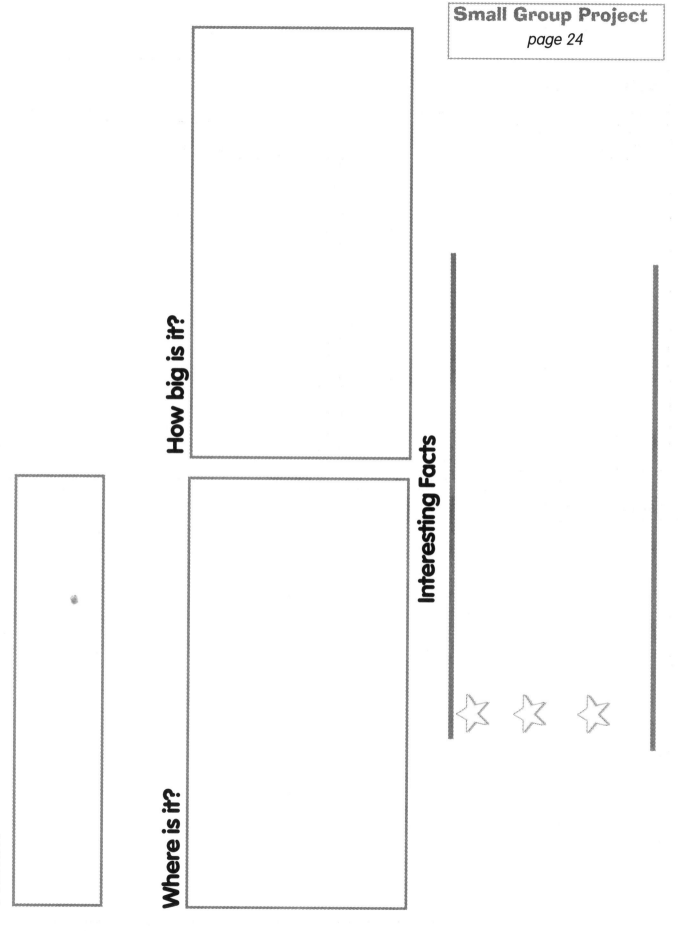

63

Planet Postcard

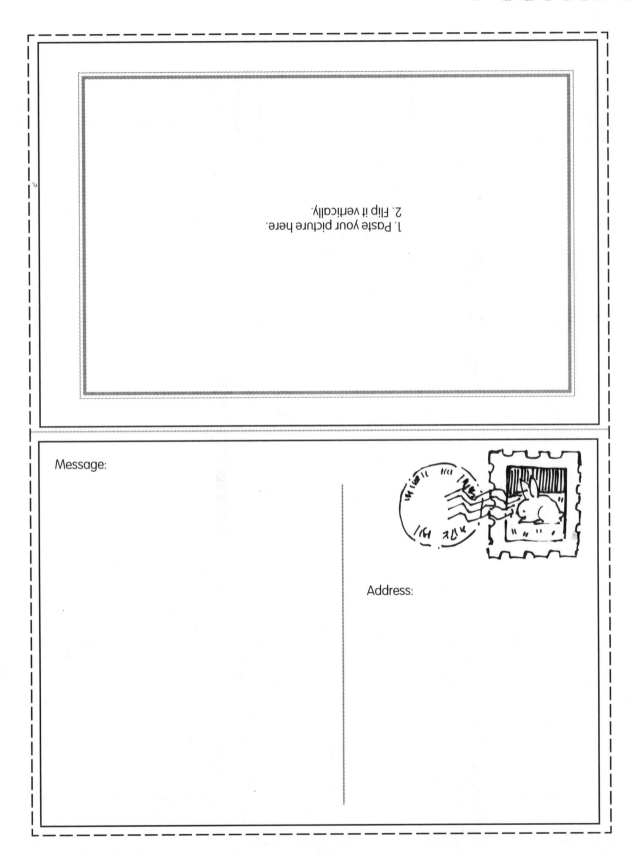

1. Paste your picture here.
2. Flip it vertically.

Message:

Address:

Activities Using the World Wide Web EMC 066

Whole Class Project

page 28

K	W	L
What We Know	What We Want to Know	What We Learned

	Where it lives	What it eats	What it looks like	Interesting facts
Reptile				• • •
Amphibian				• • •
Mammal				• • •

Name: _____

Name of animal:

_____

Circle one: Mammal   Amphibian   Reptile   Bird

Where it lives:	What it eats:	What it looks like:

Interesting facts:

Name: _____

Name of animal:

_____

Circle one: Mammal   Amphibian   Reptile   Bird

Where it lives:	What it eats:	What it looks like:

Interesting facts:

Name: _____

Name of animal:

Habitat:

Food:

Appearance:

Interesting Facts:

Name of state:

Name:

This is...

Time Line for a Famous House

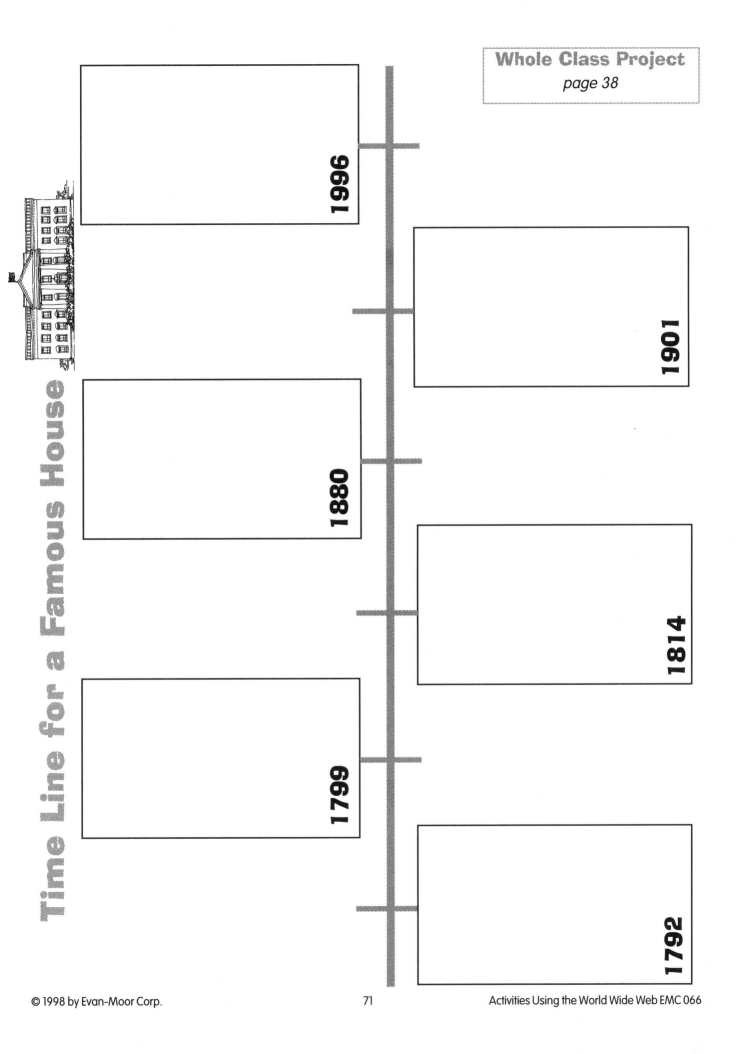

1996

1901

1880

1814

1799

1792

Activities Using the World Wide Web EMC 066

White House Floor Plan

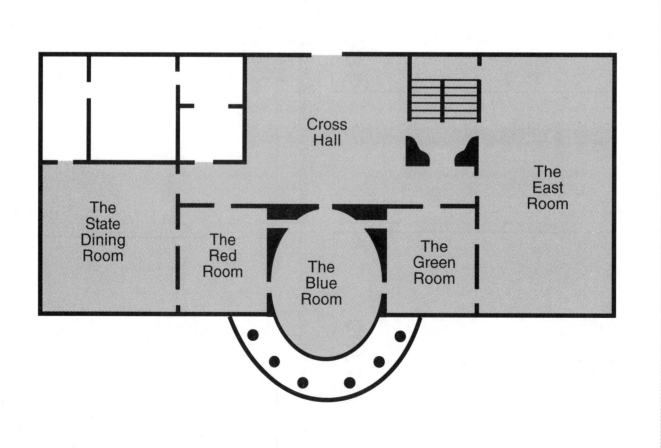

The Green Room

The Blue Room

The Red Room

The State
Dining Room

The East Room

Living in the White House

by

Activities Using the World Wide Web EMC 066

Name of Native American tribe:	Region where they live(d):
	Put a mark on the map to show the region.

Interesting Facts

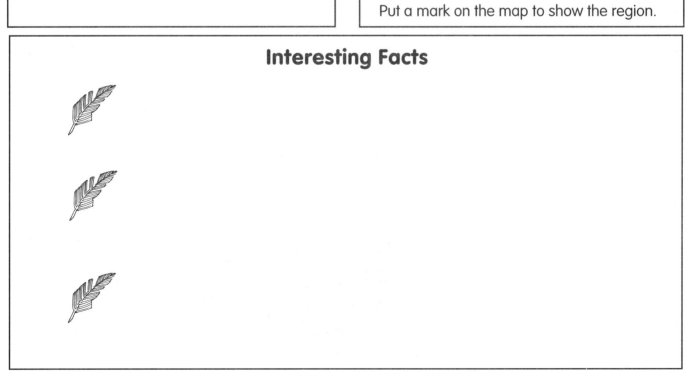

Tribe:

Where They Live(d)

Contributions

Important Facts in Their History

The Tribe Today

Source of information:

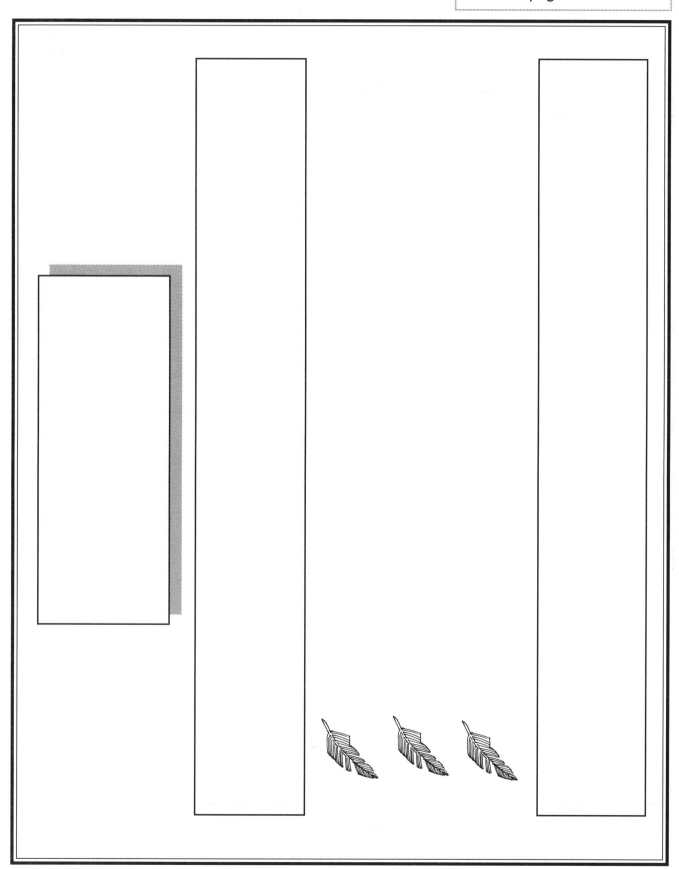

Checklist of Computer Skills

Student Names	Identify computer parts	Open hard drive	Open programs	Open a bookmark	Search for information (use subject directory)	Search for information (use key words)	Add a bookmark	Click mouse	Double-click mouse	Point	Use a scroll bar	Draw	Choose tool	Fill with color	Select and copy	Keyboard	Respect and care for computers

Dear Parents,

Using the computer as a tool for learning is an important part of our curriculum. We are able to find up-to-date information on the World Wide Web. Sometimes the information looks like the text in a book. Sometimes it is an illustration or a photograph. Sometimes it is a movie, a speech, or a sound. We use the information that we find to learn about all the different things that we are studying. Here is a research activity that your child completed.

Ask your child to tell you about how he or she used the World Wide Web to find information.

Thank you for your help and your interest the in World Wide Web resources that your child is accessing.

Sincerely,

Teaching and Learning
with the
Computer

Dear Parents,

Using the computer as a tool for learning is an important part of our curriculum. We are able to find up-to-date information on the World Wide Web. Sometimes the information looks like the text in a book. Sometimes it is an illustration or a photograph. Sometimes it is a movie, a speech, or a sound. We use the information that we find to learn about all the different things that we are studying. Here is a research activity that your child completed.

Ask your child to tell you about how he or she used the World Wide Web to find information.

Thank you for your help and your interest the in World Wide Web resources that your child is accessing.

Sincerely,

Teaching and Learning
with the
Computer

I use
the World Wide Web
for research!

Name:

I use
the World Wide Web
for research!

Name:

I use
the World Wide Web
for research!

Name:

I use
the World Wide Web
for research!

Name: